# INFIDELITIES

# Infidelities

### Poems by Sonia Farmer

POINCIANA PAPER PRESS

Published by Poinciana Paper Press
Nassau, The Bahamas

Copyright © 2017 by Sonia Farmer

No part of this book can be reproduced in any form without permission in writing from the publisher

Book design by Sonia Farmer

Book cover image used under license from Shutterstock.com, designed and originally letterpress-printed by Sonia Farmer in a first edition of 300 copies

Title page image is *Poinciana* from *Flore des serres et jardins de Paris*, 1834, by P.C. Van Geel

ISBN 978-0-9989150-0-5

# Contents

The Conception of Anne Bonny  *1*
The Limits of the Earth  *3*
The Marriage of Anne Bonny  *5*
Captain Johnson  *6*
Anne Sets Fire to the Plantation  *7*
It Begins with Rejection  *8*
Anne on the High Sea  *9*
The Effect of Fire on Memory  *10*
Take It or Take It Back  *11*
Calico  *12*
Some Marry Seasons  *13*
Capturing Fire  *14*
The Seamonster Will Not Move in with You  *15*
Not Waving  *16*
Severing Ties  *17*
The Seamonster Is Not a Stalker  *18*
Once  *19*
Capturing Water  *20*
Hellcat  *21*
Suddenly  *22*
Homeward  *23*

Sirenomelia  25
In Sickness, in Health  26
The Seamonster's Existential Crisis  28
Black Poui  29
The Seamonster on the Shore  30
The Other Woman  31
The Seamonster Is Not a Bridezilla  32
Shot in Hell  33
Post Script  34
Last Words  35
The Seamonster Goes to Bed Angry  36
The Tryal  37
Offerings Material  46
A Letter from Paradise  48
A Letter from Home  49
The Trial  50
Reunion  52
The Seamonster Is Not Lonely  53
Queen Anne's Revenge  54

Acknowledgements  56

*for Allan Murray*

# THE CONCEPTION OF ANNE BONNY

In one version,
Anne's father impregnates
the housekeeper.
His wife takes her to court,
exiles her to the colonies.
Anne's father follows.

Displacement: to swear
the color of the water
changes. New voices
murmur from the sea.
The skin adopts
new salt and water languages
and speaks them, softens.

It is easy
for the man to recover
his social stature
when displaced
to the colonies.

In Carolina all you need
is money, a plantation,
a clapboard house with a porch,
and a good family.

Displacement: the color
of the world changes.
Why bother with light?
The pitch of the home
defined by the lack
of his shirts hanging
on chair backs.

Says the dusty table: *Do not
set places for three:
there was never anything
worth your womb.*

The bed: *Your existence
will never again be defined
by the body sleeping
next to you.*

*Did you think
this was a closet?*
the sink asks the
sleepwalker.

The sleepwalker stares
at the sink:
*My dreams promised me
an ocean.*

# THE LIMITS OF THE EARTH

Subtract all the sand grains
I've swallowed,
the maps of moles burned
on my back.

Subtract the resilient scrubby brush
making the sweetest fruit
out of salty air and chalky soil.

Subtract that long
wet season after so many
dry years.
Subtract the mango trees
weighed down
with the heaviest fruit
I had ever seen.

Subtract the royal poincianas,
their red petals inextinguishable
even by the violent
fingers of rain.

You don't know about
the poincianas, their triumph
during the long dry spell—
you had never seen a tree
on fire. I tried to explain:

Sometimes we have to chose.
By that I mean: I am a woman.

I have set many fires before you
And since then I have been
putting them out.

Nothing can teach me more
than the island has taught me.

# THE MARRIAGE OF ANNE BONNY

Anne spends the week following her beating of a suitor inside as punishment. A young servant girl watches her. Though you are not familiar with Anne yet, you will soon know that she would not tolerate this for long. How else could she have met her future husband, James Bonny, if she did not escape the confines of her father's plantation?

She makes her way into town. She wonders how to escape from the marriage she knows will soon come. Her husband will leave her for another, just as her father left the woman he married. This she knows is inevitable: daughters always become their mothers, because their mothers always become their grandmothers. But what if she didn't?

She smiles at James. He takes her white hand. Her hand that held the kitchen knife still tangled in the abdomen of the slave girl, the slave girl whose mother's knived body fell also, long ago.

## CAPTAIN JOHNSON

Portray her as feisty as
her actions.
Explain her:

The death of thirteen. A
dinner knife. A suitor.

We need biological
justification. Women
possess strange selves.

Claim abnormality. Some
masculine feature.
Some strange
displacement.

Remember
the need to separate
the self.
Move away.
Resist daily
the surface
of the mirror.

A figure floats there.
He has your
god-given hands.

## ANNE SETS FIRE TO THE PLANTATION

Like the best of criminals hidden in clear sight, Anne learned how to break the rules through a well-versed knowledge of law and order passed down from one privileged generation to the next.

Thanks to her father, Anne knew the names and positions of all dining spoons, how deep to curtsey, how to properly address letters, the particular rules of bridge. In her free time she used the deck of cards folded in half to build elaborate houses, pockets the queen of hearts. Then she dismantles it with one purse of her lips, places the queen on top. She is not ungrateful for these lessons.

When she was a girl she preferred to address her letters in fire red. Is there joy in imitation? With a bag slung over her left shoulder and a heart burning in her pocket, she grips a lantern loaded with oil in her hand, wedding band flickering fearlessly on her finger. She curtseys for the last time. *Dear father,*

*Look upon your field in flames. I am your daughter. I was your daughter.*

## IT BEGINS WITH REJECTION

I had to exist somewhere
with more than one season.
I had to move away
from the fire to crave it.

I had to taste the salt
mixed in a cup of water
in the silence of winter,
cold spoon against colder glass.

How else could I know
what is imitation, what is reality?

## ANNE ON THE HIGH SEA

Against her father's training and wishes, Anne marries the sailor and leaves for Nassau. Her defiance is marked by marrying into the lowest level of society. We understand a child always strives to become the opposite of its parents. It must leave their home to find reasons to return. *Already,* she thinks, *I am proving to be the opposite of my mother: alive.*

# THE EFFECT OF FIRE ON MEMORY

Here, on the tip of the ocean's tongue, it is always summer.

Anne stands under a poinciana in her garden and catches the tiny red petals in her pale hand. Her husband, watching her, feels a strange jealousy as she pockets these small fires. He had seen her once tangled and coy in a shower of weeping willows. Only scorched earth remains there, in her memory. After all, these trees do not weep; they burn.

## TAKE IT OR TAKE IT BACK

I am rethinking this today:
the stove that doesn't light,
the live-in mouse, the
life defined by you and
four seasons forever.

There is no room in my body
for orange leaves, for snow;
there is too much fire
and salt and I'm not
giving them up for you yet.

You will have to build
our house out of ice.
You will have to forgive me
when I destroy it.

No quick or dramatic
displays. No flames, I promise.
Just a slow melt.
You won't even realize it
until it is too late.

You will wake up one day,
and you will understand.
My infidelities
will have changed you.

## CALICO

We are not sure how Anne Bonny met Jack Rackham.

In one version, she becomes a harlot, frequenting bars and tempting pirates wandering through Nassau.

She thinks harlot thoughts like:

*I actively forget the laundry on the line.*
*I actively forget the rooms, the corners of my house.*

This is the way we prepare to belong to the sea.

She walks past bars toward the docked ships. If you had asked her she will tell you she did not see his face first. She did not see his hand reach out to touch the flame of her hair.

She saw flowers. She saw them come at her and she surrendered herself to them as she will surrender herself to him:
whole.

## SOME MARRY SEASONS

Here again, the trees dying
from the top down,
while others prefer
an all-over suffering.

Watching, I am as helpless
as the plant who gives up
their last leaf.

I've never seen such
public announcements,
save for the women
in clapboard houses who
allow the laundry
on the line
to soak in the rain and
remain for hours afterward;

Save for these women once telling me,
*Some women don't marry men.*
*Some of them marry places.*

# CAPTURING FIRE

Anne knows her second infidelity to her husband lies in Jack. The first lies in the poinciana. As she and her husband neared Nassau it seemed as if the horizon were on fire. He stood no chance. She was ready to belong to this place forever.

She wants to think the trees thought so, too, when they saw these limestone islands like crooked teeth framing the ocean's tongue. *Let's stay. Let's taste this salty mouth.* But she knows better. She knows a man brought the plant to the Caribbean. How like Prometheus he must have felt, clutching that first red petal in his hand, and then, giving it his name, a home among his own perfect teeth.

She imagines he sat on the grass beneath that tree in Madagascar, his head bent all the way back. He thinks: *It is so easy to love you. It is so easy to take you with me, to make you mine.* Later, he would literally set a forest alight to keep this beloved discovery to himself.

Anne can see both the ocean and the light of the scarlet tree from her kitchen window. It is not easy to love many things at once as she does. It is not fit for a woman. She knows men are allowed to love something and take it with them.

She knows the moment Jack saw her he thought, *You are such a beautiful flower. It is so easy to make you mine, to have you live in only my eyes, in only my mouth.*

She knows these were not thoughts. These were promises: *I can make you love the ocean. I can make you love me more.*

# THE SEAMONSTER WILL NOT MOVE IN WITH YOU

If you want to love me,
the ocean must never know my infidelity.

The only way to surpass the ocean
is to become it.
It is a slow but possible process,
a ritual rubbing of salt,
of swallowing sand, of sinking.

You have to imagine how to feel
the smallest changes in your blood.
Blood and seawater are almost
chemically identical. Only a few
simple adjustments are needed
to unlock that evolutionary memory.

Don't despair, my love—
once you follow me into the blackest part
of the deep, your blood will understand
what needs to happen.

## NOT WAVING

Don't you ever forget
that you are mine. I claim
you and every crooked tooth,
the mole hidden behind
your earlobe. Everything.
I claim even the open water
of your dreams.

Even though history tells us
women are not to claim men
as their own, did you think
Kalypso would just build Odysseus
that ship and stand by
with a heart sick with sorrow?

Do not forget she clothed the hero
before he set out to sea.
These clothes later sucked him down
enraged stormy water:
*If you are not mine then*
*no one shall claim you.*

## SEVERING TIES

When Jack offered to purchase Anne from her husband, they were denied. Jack's punishment was banishment. Anne's was public flogging. When you give yourself whole to a man who is not your husband—nevermind the trickery of flowers—you will always end up in pieces.

Anne's husband must have forgotten the spirit of the woman he married. He does not think, as he sees her return from the town square, bruised as a crushed hibiscus, that she has already decided to leave him as she left her father: by the ocean.

She waits until the poincianas bloom again. And then, she will wake up and glance outside her window and see a figure in the shade of the flame tree, staring back. The figure leaves a red flower on her windowsill. She wears this in her hair the whole day, but not even this will signal to her husband to seek higher ground from the surge of her sucked-back rage.

It is only after she steals his clothing, only after she follows the figure that reappears at dusk to the dock full of sleeping ships, only after she holds a gun to the head of a guard while the figure leads his crew on board, that he will come home

to a particular underwater silence, as if the house had been buried by a tidal wave long ago, and he will find in every single impeccable room, like a most poisonous infiltration of sea anemone, those red flowers tangled with the severed strands of her hair.

## THE SEAMONSTER IS NOT A STALKER

Love, I am good at waiting.
Once, I may have been a lighthouse wife
or I may have been a lighthouse.
You will find me on the darkest night
aflame on the horizon
casting nets of light on the backs of waves:
love letters written in salted braille ready
to crack away from the waves broken by
the ribs of your most faithful ship
and find their way on deck where
you stand, mouth wide open and hungry
to feel the tongue of the ocean
meet your own once more.

ONCE

Onto the walls of your room,
the windows bleed sunrise

into a whiteness,
until there are no windows—

until the walls themselves
become light.

Outside, a glass building
resists becoming the sky.

At that moment you part
my hair at an unfamiliar place.

You say,
*You are such a beautiful flower.*

You say,
*It is so easy to love you.*

I know
what comes next

out of that wicked
prison of a mouth.

# CAPTURING WATER

For that year Jack took to sea before returning for her, Anne must have visited the ocean daily to prepare herself for what she knew was coming.

She would get used to sand on her feet, then on her entire skin. She would fill her shoes with those grains so she could learn their names by weight; she would memorize the song of each seashell like a woman who knows which lover's bed she lies in by the pitch of his breath as he descends into the open sea of his dreams.

She would then enter the ocean—a day for toes, another for ankles, two for knees—until her mouth watered for salt, her eyes knew burning subsided, and her skin knew the names of each wave breaking on her back.

She could almost breathe underwater by the time Jack returned. But we know better. We know the ocean doesn't just submit like that, and we know a woman is always aware she is being watched.

What happened was there would be whole days devoted to watching her roll on shore. Whole days devoted to speaking to her skin. Eventually and inevitably, there would just be devotion.

# HELLCAT

Displacement becomes apparent,
tides of anger rolling
in and out of our bodies.

I throw a suitcase
out of the front door—
we challenge the silence
of absence, the space
that asks, inevitable:
*Who are you now if not
defined by another?*

I know that in the brain
love is not defined
by the absence of its other.
They share the same space.

The tide of light
leaving just beyond
your windowsill
brings me home.

This does not mean
I love you.
This means I now
have the language
to hate you
in the act of returning.

# SUDDENLY

Jack was right about one thing. He did make Anne love the ocean. But she is not sure that she loves him more, and this is her first infidelity to him.

For a while it seemed as if she were in a dream, a dream where she is not herself. She wakes up and looks in the mirror, stifles a curtsey: *pleased to meet you*. This is how she continues to live in third person.

She sees her legs in men's pants and her hands clutching a cutlass and blood that doesn't come from her body. She is good at swearing and holding her liqueur but she is best at killing up close. She bathes in the sea fully clothed until she is alone and Jack makes sure no one asks the wrong questions.

But the dreamer always wakes up. One day she realizes blood doesn't come from her anymore. She pulls Jack aside and removes her clothes in a way that they will not lay together and he places his hand on her swollen belly.

He makes promises about Cuba. He tells her about a house on the shore and swears this will be enough and she begins to live in a different dream. But she knows better. She knows that when a man lives with the ocean this long, the ship becomes a home. It becomes a home after it becomes a wife.

## HOMEWARD

It's hard to understand
the act of leaving;
even harder the act
of returning.

Deep in the heart of
a foreign city,
all I do is witness
the stripping of trees.

I imagine
what it must be like
to die twice:
once at the first sign
of earth's betrayal
and again at
the bright green desire
to be part of the
forgotten landscape
once more,
as if loss
had never changed me.

Bury loss within.
This is necessary.
This is how
you begin to belong
to the first spring

after I leave you
without any buried
bulbs in my wake,

just strands of my hair
tucked into the corners
of your home—

yes, my love,
into every single one.

## SIRENOMELIA

There's never a happy ending to this chapter. No records of Anne's child exist. In one version, Anne leaves it. In another version, it is stillborn.

In this version, Anne must have played house with Jack for months only to wake from that dream with childbirth.

She clutches a stained bundle of sheets and wails. A large wave breaking onto the sand can be heard in a roar just outside the window: *Are you ready to return to me?*

She opens the door and lets the sea take the sheets, and then the child with a fused tail, and then herself. She hopes what they say about the sea and grief is true: that bathing in a leaving tide will wash the sadness straight out of your soul.

She lights a candle every night in the window of the house on the shore. It is a lighthouse, she decides. That is to say, it is a tombstone. Nothing returns to shore as whole as it left.

## IN SICKNESS, IN HEALTH

If Nassau had a spring it would be now.
The poor-man's-orchid is in bloom,
and the bougainvillea begin
their thorny ascent up white trellises.
It is too early for the poinciana—
their pods, those foot-long
woman's tongues, rattle against
bare branches.

As my mother loads her car,
I watch a coffin slipped
into a hearse filled with flowers.
*The dead watch over us,* she says.
We believe such things here.
A suited man admires the printed poppies
of my dress from afar. I sense his smile.
A stranger's smile or greeting
instills dread, a leftover caution
of the city. I try to smile back.

I try not to miss things
like a joneser standing at
my car window, like
the potcakes wasting away beneath
parked trucks, like
the women in supermarkets with
last night's curlers still tangled in their hair.
The city's blindness drops away,
but the grief I have pulled
into myself does not—
just exchanges with this remorse
like water through my gills.

On the road we pass three funerals.
I know not from gatherings
of overwhelming black, but from color—
grief takes many shades,
we believe such things here.
Participants wait for the hearse
under a bare silk cotton tree—the tree of spirits.
An Easter breeze lifts a woman's magenta hat
from her bowed head. I hear the click
of woman's tongues—those
who have married the island, this earth: *You
will know it as I know it.*

# THE SEAMONSTER'S EXISTENTIAL CRISIS

Subtract my name; I don't
really exist. Floating in nothing,
I am a myth, a memory
of the sea—a seamonster.
How fitting, seamonsters
only have lovers, no mothers,
no children. Or maybe their children
are the waves, the nameless
waves. Maybe the seamonster
does not bother to learn
each name and maybe the waves
don't bother to learn hers.
In this way it's almost like she
doesn't exist. And so I don't
exist. You don't love me.
You don't love anything at all.

## BLACK POUI

It is the day to return to sea.

Jack shutters the Cuban house and waits at the dock with a new crew. Anne searches the garden like she used to in Nassau for her beloved poincianas, but all she finds to sit beneath now is a black poui.

*I should drown in flowers. I should drag me down.*

She is waking up from a long dream, stemming back to the ocean, back to Nassau, back to Carolina, back even to the Irish landscape she has never seen. Did the flaming trees exist? Her head bent all the way back.

*Tree of water, tree of dusk, what is left for me but this?*

A slow reply: dusk falls, petal by violet petal, extinguishing everything.

When Jack unearths her later he will find her changed. She will return to sea dressed as a man but she will not cut her hair. She will let them ask all the wrong questions because she will be better at killing. She will learn to live in first person.

Because of her, they will become famous and famous they will become hunted.

She knows that to be a pirate one must be a man, and she does not want to be a man. So she will not be another pirate. She will be Anne Bonny.

## THE SEAMONSTER ON THE SHORE

The ocean will not talk to me anymore.
It felt me leaving, Anne's ritual in reverse:
The salt flaking away, the sand washed off.

The ocean swallows my footprints
not in the way we sometimes feel
the need to make the things we love a part of us
but by way of saying *I have never known you.*

I scour the shore daily for a letter in a bottle,
some salted Braille left behind in the sand,
a shell to press against my ear and hear
the jealous beckoning of a place that has
not yet forgotten me.

Instead the sea vomits tires,
beer bottle caps, indistinguishable plastic
debris, tangled green nets, even dead whales.
And then one day I cut my foot
on the edge of half a clear glass bottle,
a perfectly intact miniature ship inside
making its escape.

## THE OTHER WOMAN

We are not sure when exactly Anne met fellow disguised female pirate Mary Read. They may have met on Nassau, or they may have met when Jack's crew intercepted a Dutch merchant ship.

In one version, they have an affair. This is a limited understanding of what would become a relationship so complex, even Calico Jack could not crack it.

Anne stares at the young man signing the ships records. She is remembering her dream, the one where she is another who is part of her. Is she in love with Mark Read? Is Mark Read in love with her?

They decipher each other's faces. Anne thinks of a diver's feet burned by fire coral. A bird tucked under the arm of a wave. The struggle of seaweed. She touches Mark's face and Mark tries to say he is Mary but nothing comes out because they both know what they see in the lines of their faces and it needs no words. The others they may call it sun damage but these two they know well the consequences of desire.

## THE SEAMONSTER IS NOT A BRIDEZILLA

And then I realize there
are times I imagine my wedding,
imagine dancing, imagine
the settings, the blazing trees. It

will be June maybe, July maybe.
It will follow the blooming. And
then I realize the faces that should
be there are not the faces I

imagine and even his face
even that is not the same and then I realize
I'm not sure what faces if any are
there. Maybe there are no faces. The

harder I search for them the more
they disappear until they are all blank,
until even the setting is blank,
extinguished as if they had been

eroded by sea waves or perhaps the
waves of my mind—yes, those nameless
waves making nameless faces, faceless
faces receding like waves.

## SHOT IN HELL

When authorities surrounded Jack's sloop, he and his crew hid away, drunk, below deck. Anne and Mary alone fought, all guns and cutlasses before their capture.

This is what history tells us. It also tells us the words accompanying Anne's gunshot into the hold: *If there's a man among ye, ye'll come up and fight.*

And the shot of language itself?
Or silence, that fatal bullet:

*Won't you who have pledged love to me save me—or are you not my other?*

## POST SCRIPT

Either I'm not learning
this language fast enough,
or you've remembered
how to turn away.

Last night, your voice
came through scattered
on my screen. The lost
letters stolen by distance
have gathered between us.
We can't speak now
as a rule, but we haven't really
been speaking for some time.

For some time, I have felt you
wash out to sea without
the anchor of my voice.
How does it feel to be
without an anchor? That
is how I feel every day.

## LAST WORDS

Anne spoke to Jack before his hanging. He had requested her visit, expecting perhaps some farewell filled with grief.

Instead, there she was, saying: *I am sorry to see you here, Jack, but if you had fought like a man, you needn't hang like a dog.*

Not saying: *That gunpowder mixed with rum, didn't we have it together? Didn't we make promises?*

Not saying, with an aftertaste of gunpowder bubbling from the base of her gut: *I now have the language to hate you in the act of returning, and I give it to you as you have given it to me.*

## THE SEAMONSTER GOES TO BED ANGRY

Leave everything
you know. You have
permission. Leave our
present world. Sleep
on different shores of
dreams. Count perfect
waves. I refuse
to hit you. I refuse
the distance. Where feet
graze the sand, you
no longer have permission.
I cannot sleep, perfect
waves, I refuse.

# THE TRYAL

*Mary Read, Ann Bonny,* alias
*Bonn*

the Register exhibited the Articles against them; which he read to them in the following words

against
> *Mary Read* and *Ann Bonny*, alias *Bonn*, late of the
> Island of Providence Spinsters

*Mary Read* and *Anne Bonny,* alias
*Bonn,* and each of them

    upon the high Sea, in a certain Sloop
                  feloniously and wickedly

On the high Sea   in execution of their said
Evil Designs                             (to wit)

    Upon the high Sea, in a certain Place

Piratically, feloniously

                                                  (

aforesaid unknown)                    Piratically,
Feloniously

                                (whose names

       aforesaid unknown)                                  in
the peace of God
Piratically, and Felo-
niously

                         in Corporal Fear of their Lives
             piratically and feloniously

there upon
the high Sea aforesaid, in the aforesaid place


upon the high Sea
aforesaid, in the place aforesaid

              *to wit*
the said *Mary Read*, and
*Ann Bonny*, alias *Bonn*, and each of them
Upon the high
Sea, in a certain place

                                Piratically and Feloniously

   (     aforesaid                      unknown)

        Piratically, and Feloniously

      (whose names                                                             aforesaid are
unknown)                                                                 in the peace of
God
Piratically, and Feloni
ously

         in Corporal fear of their Lives

upon the high Sea, the place
aforesaid

the said *Mary Read*, and *Anne Bonny*,
alias *Bonn*, and each of them
                  (to wit)

                            Upon the high sea, at a certain place

Piratically, Feloniously, and in an Hostile manner

            (         aforesaid unknown)
Piratically, Feloniously, and in an Hostile
manner
                                     (whose Names
aforesaid are unknown)
in the Peace of God

Piratically and
Feloniously

                in Corporal fear of their Lives
                Piratically and Feloniously


the said *Mary Read*, and *Ann Bonny*,
alias *Bonn*, and each of them
      (*to wit*)
upon the
high Sea, at a certain place

Pirati-
Cally, Feloniously, and in an Hostile manner

                              (

aforesaid unknown)


   (whose Names               aforesaid are unknown)
in the Peace of God

                    Piratically, and Feloniously


In Corporal Fear of their
Lives                           Piratically, and Feloniously

pleaded, *Not Guilty*

Then the Register did call and produce Witness

And they deposed as follows

Two Women, Prisoners at the Bar
wore Mens Jackets

cursed and swore at the Men

That the reason of knowing and believing them
to be Women then was, by the largeness of their Breasts

the two Women, Prisoners at the
Bar




                                                                    Two
                                                      Women, Prisoners at the Bar



handed Gun-powder to the
Men
They wore Men's Cloaths; and, at other Times, they
wore Women's Cloaths      they did not seem to be kept,
or detain'd by Force, but of their own Free-Will



              two Women, Prisoners at the Bar

had no
Witnesses, nor any Questions to ask

And they, nor either of them, offering any Thing material, his Excellency the President, pronounced Sentence of Death upon them in the Words following


*Go*
*from hence to the Place from whence you came*




*quick with child, and pray*

## OFFERINGS MATERIAL

two women
prisoners   at the bar

are here to    witness your
grand firing    of tongues

do you have    witness or
any questions to   ask

then   go from   hence
to the place    from

whence   you came with
nothing but    your memories

which will
betray  you

and your    voice
clear    with longing

but do not    forget us    sirs
how can you

how can you    forget
the thing    you once possessed

it still    exists    out there
without you

a beloved    blinking
horizon light

you can't    approach it
it    marks a graveyard

ask us    how we know
ask us    what we have buried

to love    in the way we did
piratically    feloniously

upon    a dear high sea
and below    a dear high sea

when you    kiss
the tongue of    the ocean

it will    wreck you
a    scattered debris    of

insatiable desire
we will    tell you    a secret

the difference    between waves
is one breaks    and one    takes

and one moves
a shoreline    so slowly

you    will think    your memories
have    betrayed you

ask us    which ones
we are

## A LETTER FROM PARADISE

A dilapidated greenhouse lies
in the frame of my window.
Inside, bushes of white hibiscus
come forward each day. The morning
unfurls them, spilling cream,
white hands opening to whiter palms,
to blood-red centers. These
small fires alight, burn brilliant
white holes through my retina, through
the day, spots that do not out.
The evening does not bring
a closing. No, we will know
what we have lost. Each corolla drops
to the evening ground. What's done
will not be undone. You wanted
to know: That
is how each day passes here.

## A LETTER FROM HOME

Today I knew where I was
when I woke. A brightness behind
my lids. The fire of morning
through the gauze of white curtain.
A fierce breeze straight from the mouths
of waves. Unstoppable. I'm sorry
for the things I've said. I know
you subtracted me long ago.
Please take me back.

## THE TRIAL

I can always tell us apart
in airport lines.
It is best if we not
let ourselves be known;
those tied to an island
don't know how to
see it the right way.

I plead guilty—I do not see it
a bright flashy poster way,
a scattered cartoon logo way,
an endless sandy beach way.

I plead guilty to hating
the tourist girl there
with perfect teeth
in love after a five-day-four-night
honeymoon—saying
*love* as if she were versed
in the many shapes
of it, the many weights of it.

How smooth her words are,
how sharp mine—how much
they cut my mouth, get stuck
in my throat.

Little girl, have you ever
bitten down on a conch pearl?
Love here is like that: sometimes
you lose things—

or else the ugly slug of your tongue
makes from all the sharp
little words an unexpectedly
perfect globe of desire,
and then another and another,
until you wear this longing
around your neck.

The island is not your lover
until it has broken your teeth
then asked you to stay a while longer
while you hang yourself with
its gifts.

I plead guilty to conspire:
once, a lover pressed his mouth
to the phone and said
*come back*, but I could not hear him.
I heard only the ocean in my ears
and felt only these salty sighs
breaking on my teeth.

I plead guilty to placing the sand
in his shoes one grain at a time,
day by day; I plead guilty
to knowing it would only end
with our underwater words:
*I never meant to flood your house,*
*I only meant to drown it.*

# REUNION

No records exist about Anne's execution. No records exist about her exit from Jamaica, or birth of her second child, or her death.

In one version, a romantic version, she continues pirating. In another, her father ransoms her and places her back onto a domestic trajectory.

Perhaps a guard recognized her, as her father remained a powerful figure in the colonies well after Anne's departure.

She may have imagined his life continuing elsewhere, as the many ghosts of her possible lives continue elsewhere. Or maybe she never thought of him. Maybe the memory of his face burned away like his plantation the day she left.

She meets her father somewhere safe, perhaps under a silk cotton tree whose spring pods she watched from the pale square of a window in her cell. She does not know why the young guard has dragged her here at dusk. And then, the figure approaching her, the figure outlined by light falling like cotton, light falling like a thousand feathers.

She and her father stand face to face. She wants to say: *I am your daughter. I became you. Look at my burned face.* She wants to say: *You are only the next ticket on my journey. You are only a piece falling into place.*

But instead she turns her face to the twisting branches, sees the cotton alighting from pods there, the cotton she thought was light. She cranes her neck and the sun falls across it, and her father sees the light in the shape of scales turning to feathers, and she knows a change is coming. She cannot see his face. It is ablaze. Or maybe it is her eyes. The light of her eyes. Or maybe the light of her mind. Yes. Maybe leaving has changed her.

# THE SEAMONSTER IS NOT LONELY

There is no in-between. Either I love
the way that ships love—throwing
themselves upon the Devil's Backbone—
or I love the way that treacherous shoal loves,
sending splinters of hundreds of spent ships
to every shore. Either way, the object
of affection remains the island.

Perhaps only lighthouses know the truth.
Perhaps if I stay in one place long enough,
maybe I too will discover the reason
for the whale's temporary and mad desire
to try its luck on shore.

Perhaps if I keep completely still,
I can call back those splinters from
their graves to build with them a ship
in a bottle, throw it towards that lighthouse—
that lighthouse filled with spring.

# QUEEN ANNE'S REVENGE

Anne scans the horizon. She is not looking for anything. She is seeing, in her mind's eye, the ravaged ship behind her that gave her crew loot. She knows this because of the heat. Prayers. She did this. A ship-shaped fire. She sees it. Everything fades. She is waiting for the complete vision, the pieces falling together, like listening for a flower opening, the weight of the air shifting, until it is done, and then one can replay it as quickly as one likes, a tiny explosion of the mind, over and over. The blossoming of the brain. Of the tree. Of the tree on fire. Smoldering. Yes. She sees it. She sees a ship-shaped fire. It is and isn't her.

# *Acknowledgements*

I am so grateful to the editors of the following journals who published previous versions of poems in this collection:

"Severing Ties" in *POUi: Cave Hill Journal of Creative Writing* (The University of West Indies, Vol. XI, December 2010); "Anne Destroys the Plantation" and "The Effect of Fire on Memory" in *The Caribbean Writer* (University of the Virgin Islands, Vol. 24, 2010); "Calico", "Capturing Fire", "Capturing Water", "Suddenly", "Sirenomelia", "Black Poui", "The Other Woman", "Reunion", and "Queen Anne's Revenge" in *WomanSpeak: A Journal of Writing and Art by Caribbean Women* (Vol. 5, 2010); and "The Conception of Anne Bonny" (June 2009) and "Last Words", "The Seamonster Is Not a Bridezilla", "The Tryal" (February 2012) online in *tongues of the ocean*.

I'd also like to extend gratitude to *Small Axe* for awarding a selection of these poems with joint first place in poetry in their 2011 Literary Competition and for publishing them in Volume 16, Number 2, in July 2012: "It Begins with Rejection", "The Limits of the Earth", "Some Marry Seasons", "Take It or Take It Back", "Hellcat", "The Trial", "In Sickness, in Health", "A Letter from Paradise", "Post-Script", and "The Seamonster Isn't Lonely" (previously "Homing").

Additionally, "The Tryal" and "Offerings Material" appeared in the interactive art project "Making Waves", exhibited at Doongalik Studios in Nassau, The Bahamas as part of the 2014 Transforming Spaces art tour. Thank you Pam and Orchid Burnside, and the TS committee, for that exhibition space, and thank you to those who participated by giving witness.

This collection could not have been possible without a lifetime of teachers who pushed me to write and read and who inspired me with their own work. To them I am eternally grateful: Cathy Roach, Angela Darville, Jennifer Taylor, Sarah Manguso, Samantha Hunt, Christian Hawkeye, Anna Moschovakis, Helen Klonaris, and Obediah Michael Smith. Special thanks to the original pirate, Mr. Allan Murray. This book began in your high school history class. Finally, thank you, Julie Leonard, for giving me the tools, confidence, and advice to manifest this collection as I've always envisioned it.

Thank you to my friends and colleagues at Pratt Institute who gave thoughtful feedback to form the first draft of this body of work, and thank you to the Writing Program for awarding it with the 2009 poetry thesis award.

Thank you to the community of Caribbean writers who, through their friendship and mentorship, patiently encouraged me to share this work at my own pace: Christian Campbell, Marion Bethel, Nicolette Bethel, Lynn Sweeting, Asha Rahming, Margot Bethel, Christi Cartwright, Keisha Lynne, Nicholas Laughlin, Sharon Millar, and anyone else I may have neglected to include who may have helped to midwife this collection into being. Thank you to the Bocas Literary Festival and to the University of The Bahamas for giving me platforms to share this work.

Thank you to my parents for their unending emotional, physical, financial, spiritual, and creative support in all of my endeavors. Thank you for always validating and nurturing my tireless curiosity and for giving me the space and tools to explore my creativity. Thank you, ultimately, for always reminding me that art is a valid career path. I love you.

And of course, thank you to the man who brought out the seamonster in me so that I could form these poems.

Sonia Farmer is a writer, visual artist, and small press publisher who uses letterpress printing, bookbinding, hand-papermaking, and digital projects to build narratives about the Caribbean space. She is the founder of Poinciana Paper Press, a small independent press located in Nassau, The Bahamas, which produces handmade and limited edition chapbooks of Caribbean literature and promotes the crafts of book arts through workshops and creative collaborations. Her artwork has been exhibited throughout Nassau including at the National Art Gallery of The Bahamas. Her poetry has won the 2011 Prize in the Small Axe Literary Competition and has appeared in *tongues of the ocean, The Caribbean Writer, Poui, The WomanSpeak Journal,* and *Moko Magazine.* She holds a BFA in Writing from Pratt Institute.

www.ingramcontent.com/pod-product-compliance
Lightning Source LLC
Chambersburg PA
CBHW030457010526
44118CB00011B/985